Henry Benjamin Wheatley, George Laurence Gomme

Chap-books and Folk-lore Tracts

IV.

Henry Benjamin Wheatley, George Laurence Gomme

Chap-books and Folk-lore Tracts
IV.

ISBN/EAN: 9783744782425

Printed in Europe, USA, Canada, Australia, Japan

Cover: Foto ©Thomas Meinert / pixelio.de

More available books at **www.hansebooks.com**

Chap-Books
and
Folk-Lore Tracts.

Edited by

G. L. Gomme, F.S.A.

and

H. B. Wheatley, F.S.A.

———

First Series.

IV.

THE HISTORY

OF

PATIENT GRISEL.
1619.

EDITED, WITH AN INTRODUCTION,

BY

HENRY B. WHEATLEY, F.S.A.

LONDON:

PRINTED FOR THE VILLON SOCIETY.

1885.

Introduction.

THE narrative of the Patient Griselda is one of the most
wide-spread of the stories which have come down to us from
the Middle Ages. It has been annexed to the highest literature
by such poets as Boccaccio, Petrarch and Chaucer, and has been
brought within reach of the meanest capacities by the ballad-
mongers and the writers of penny histories.

We cannot trace the story back farther than the middle of
the fourteenth century, when Boccaccio incorporated it into his
Decameron (day 10, novel 10) ; but it must have had a previous
existence in Italy, for Petrarch says in his letter to Boccaccio
that when he read it in the *Decameron* he remembered how
pleased he had been with it when he heard it many years
before. When his memory was thus revived in the story that
charmed him so much he set to work to learn it by heart, so
that he might repeat it to his friends. He then translated it
into Latin for the benefit of those who did not know Italian.*

* See *Originals and Analogues of Chaucer's Canterbury Tales,* part ii. pp. 150-176
(Chaucer Society).

That he did repeat the story to his friend we learn from the
Clerk of Oxenford's Prologue to his tale in the *Canterbury
Tales*, where he says :—

> " I wil yow telle a tale, which that I
> Lerned at Padowe of a worthy clerk,
> As provyd by his wordes and his werk.
> He is now deed, and nayled in his chest,
> Now God yive his soule wel good rest !
> Fraunces Petrark, the laureat poete,
> Highte this clerk, whos rethorique swete
> Enlumynd al Ytail of poetrie."

There has been much controversy over these words. We
must all wish to believe that Chaucer met Petrarch at Padua
and was friendly with him ; but although it is highly probable
that he did so we have no actual evidence other than this
passage. Some say that Chaucer is not speaking here in his
own name but in that of a fictitious character, and therefore
the statement goes for nothing. Another objection is that here
Chaucer's indebtedness to Boccaccio is overlooked and all the
credit is given to Petrarch. It is highly probable however that
Chaucer was interested in the story from Petrarch's talk, and
that when he decided to make it one of his Canterbury Tales
he adapted it from Petrarch's translation of Boccaccio, which is
referred to farther on in the Prologue :—

> " I say that he first with heigh stole enditeth
> (Er he the body of his tale writith)

A proheme, in the which descrivith he
Piemounde, and of Saluces the contre,
And spekith of Appenyne the hulles hye,
That ben the boundes of al west Lombardye."

That this is the true origin of the Clerk's tale is confirmed
by the fact that Petrarch varied somewhat from Boccaccio's
original, and in these variations Chaucer follows Petrarch. An
impossible tale such as this requires all the art of the true poet
to make it delightful to us, and this of course we have in
Chaucer. It is far different when we come to read the
common-place prose of the chap-book or the equally common-
place verse of the ballad-monger.

The picture of patience carried to the extreme in the wife
and of brutal violence in the husband is so out of harmony with
our present views that it is somewhat difficult to read the story
with patience. We are wrong, however, in taking it in this
spirit, and Professor Hales has so beautifully expressed the true
motive of this mediæval picture that I feel I cannot do better
than transfer to these pages his remarks in the publication of
the Chaucer Society containing *Originals and Analogues of some
of Chaucer's Canterbury Tales :*—" Now, it is the characteristic
of the unsophisticated mediæval litterateur that he deals with
one idea at a time. It would often lead to a highly injurious
conclusion to attach at all equal a moral importance or rather
any moral importance to the subordinate parts of what he sets

* Part ii. 1873, p. 174.

forth. The central lesson is kept well in view; the others must look to themselves. The principal figure is brought into relief with enthusiasm; on the mere surroundings and background little or no care is spent . . . . . And so in the story of Griselda: if we would read it in the spirit of the day when it became current we should not vex ourselves into any righteous indignation against the immediate author of her most touching distresses. The old story does not make the marquis a monster in human shape; indeed, it represents him as a man of a noble and lovable nature; if he is not so, then even in the end Griselda reaps no earthly reward in permanently securing his admiration and love. And yet this marquis perpetrates inexpressible cruelties; he is a very wolf, ruthlessly teasing and tearing the gentlest of lambs. The explanation is in accordance with what has just been said: the patience of Griselda is the one theme of the tale, and nothing else is to be regarded. In relation to her the marquis has no moral being; he is a mere means of showing forth her supreme excellence; a mere mechanical expedient. He is no more morally than a thorn in the saint's footpath, or a wheel, or a cross. Surely it is vain to be wroth with him. Who rages against the mere fire that enfolds the martyr, or the nails that pierce the hands of a crucified Believer? Indeed, nothing in the tale is of any ethical moment but the carriage of the heroine herself. The eyes and the heart of the old century when she first appeared were fastened devoutly on that single form, and let all else go by. She is wifely obedience itself, nothing else. Before that virtue all other virtues bow. It enjoys a complete monopoly, an absolute sway. Other moral life is suspended in this representation of it. She has but one function ; for her there is but one sin possible, and that is to murmur. She is all meekness, all yielding, all resignation.

"Such a figure has comparatively few charms for us of these latter days. But it pleased the world once—even down to Shakespeare's time, who himself portrayed it in one of his earliest plays : Catherine in the *Taming of the Shrew* is a phase of Griselda. Perhaps in ages when much most ignorant abuse of women prevailed in literature—abuse springing mainly out of the vile prejudices and superstitions of the mediæval Church— some such figure might have been expected to arise. It is the figure of a reaction. The hearts of men refused to accept the dishonouring pictures so often drawn of their fellow mortals. They rose in a loyal insurrection against lying fables of essential wantonness and of shameful obstinacy. To such chivalrous rebels the pale, sad, constant face of Griselda showed itself as the image of far other experiences and histories; and they gazed on it as on the face of their saint. With an infinite reverence they saw her still calm and quiet in the midst of anguishes, with heart breaking but lips uttering no ill word, with eyes that through the tears with which kindly nature of herself would relieve the terrible drought of sorrow still looked nothing but inalienable tenderness and love.'

The French have claimed for their country the origination
of the story of Griselda; but their claim cannot be allowed.
The Abbé de Sade in his *Life of Petrarch* asserts that the story
is to be found in a manuscript called *Le Parement des Dames*;
but it appears that this manuscript was the work of Olivier de
la Marche, who was not born until long after the death of
Boccaccio. Boccaccio's novel was translated into French and
published at Paris about the year 1510 as *La Patience de
Grisilidis*; it was published also at Troyes about 1562. Apparently, however, the French were the first to bring Griselda
upon the stage; for, according to Warton, the Comedians of
Paris represented a mystery in French verse entitled *Le Mystere
de Griseildis, Marquis de Saluces, mis en rime françoise et par
personnaiges* in 1393. This was not printed until about 1550,
when Jehan Bonfons published it at Paris. His edition was
reprinted in 1832.

Ralph Radcliffe, a somewhat voluminous play-writer, who
flourished towards the close of the reign of Henry VIII., is
said by John Bale to have written an English comedy entitled
"Patient Griselde," and Hans Sachs in Germany converted
the story into a drama as early as 1550; but in Italy, the land
of its birth, it was not dramatised until 1620.

It was not possible for a story which had early taken such a
strong hold upon the popular imagination to remain long
without becoming the property of the ballad-writer, but we
cannot tell if he forestalled the writer of popular histories.

In the Stationers' Registers we find three entries of Griselda as early as the year 1565-6 ; the following two relate to the ballad :—

> Rd. of Owyn Rogers, for his lycense for pryntinge of a ballett intituled the sounge of pacyente Gressell unto hyr make [mate] - - - - - - - - iiij d.
> Rd. of Wylliam greffeth, for his lycense for pryntinge of ij ballettes to the tune of pacyente gressell - - iiij d.

Now the second of these entries seems to point to an earlier ballad, as it must have taken some time for the tune of Patient Grissell to become so popular ; and therefore there is great probability in Mr. Chappell's conjecture that the original ballad was published before 1557, in which year the Registers commence.

All the ballads of Griselda now in existence are essentially the same as that printed in *The Garland of Goodwill* by Thomas Deloney ; and, as the same ballad, divided into chapters with prose chapters at the beginning and end, is printed in *The Pleasant and Sweet History of Patient Grissell* (reprinted by Mr. Collier for the Percy Society), it has been suggested that this tract was also written by Deloney. This famous balladmonger is supposed to have commenced writing about the year 1586, so that it is probable that the ballad of 1565-6, and the even earlier one suggested above, have ceased to exist. The following is a list of the different titles of Deloney's ballad :—

A most pleasant Ballad of patient Grissell, to the tune of "The Bride's Good-morrow."

The earliest known edition, printed in *Collection of Seventy-nine Black-Letter Ballads and Broadsides*, 1870. P. 17. (*Roxburghe Ballads*, ed. W. Chappell, vol. ii. p. 268.)

Of Patient Grissel and a Noble Marquess. To the tune of "The Bride's Good-morrow."

T. Deloney's Garland of Good-Will. 1678. Part 2. (Percy Society. No. 112 1851.)

The earliest edition of the *Garland* must have been published before 1600, as Deloney died in that year.

A most excellent and vertuous Ballad of the Patient Grissell. To the tune of "The Bride's Good-morrow." London. Printed by John Wright. [1640?] (*Roxburghe Ballads*, vol. i. pp. 302-3.)

The first part ends—

> " My gracious Lord
> Must have his will obeyd."

And the second begins—

> " She tooke the Babies
> Even from the nursing ladies."

There is a copy of the ballad (in one, not two parts) in the Percy Folio Manuscript. See Hales and Furnivall's edition, 1868, vol. iii. p. 421.

An excellent Ballad of a Noble Marquiss and Patient Grissel. (*Collection of Old Ballads,* 1723, vol. i. p. 252.)

The following entries in the Stationers' Registers would appear to refer to the *Ancient, True, and Admirable History* printed in this volume. It is stated to be translated from the French, but this statement is of no value, and it is evidently of pure English manufacture. The edition of 1619 is the earliest known to exist :—

> 1565-6. Rd. of Thomas Colwell, for his lycense for prynting of an history of meke and pacyent Gresell - iiij d.
> 1568-9. Rd. of Thomas Colwell, for his lycense for pryntinge of the hystory of pacyent gresell, &c. - - viij d.

The History of the Noble Marquis of Salus, or Patient Grissel. Printed and sold in London. [1780 ?] 12mo. Pp. 24. Another edition. Aldermary Churchyard, n. d.

> A reduced chap-book edition of the *History* printed in this volume. It seems to have been published in this form as early as 1703.

When Mr. J. Payne Collier edited for the Percy Society " The History of Patient Grisel, two early Tracts in Black-Letter, with an Introduction and Notes," 1842, he printed after the *Ancient, True, and Admirable History* "The Pleasant and Sweet History of Patient Grissell, shewing how she from a poore man's daughter came to be a great lady of France, being a Patterne to all vertuous women. Translated out of Italian. London. Printed by E. P. for John Wright, dwelling in Giltspur Street at the Signe of the Bible."

This is divided into eleven chapters, of which 1, 2, 10, and 11, are in prose; chapters 3 to 9 contain the ballad referred to previously, and it is most probable that the whole tract was the production of Deloney. The date is cut off, but the pamphlet was probably printed about 1630, and it is doubtless a late edition of a popular chap-book. The copy in the British Museum is apparently the same as that used by Mr. Collier. It is handsomely bound in morocco, and in the inside is written in pencil, "Cost me eight pounds unbound." There are two titles : the first is "The History of the Noble Marques," with a woodcut of Griselda at the spinning-wheel. On the back of this is the woodcut of Elizabeth, reproduced on the title of the Percy Society reprint.

The play of Ralph Radcliffe is now lost, so that the comedy published in 1603 and reprinted in 1841 is the only one known to exist. We have here a curious instance of the danger of asserting of any particular book that it is unique. When Mr. Collier reprinted the play for the Shakespeare Society he said that there was no copy in the British Museum, and that the only copies he knew of were one in the Bodleian and another in the possession of the Duke of Devonshire, who also had an imperfect copy which he presented to Collier.

There is now a copy in the British Museum, and in it is this note in ink: " The only copy extant.—J. B. 1788." Under this is a pencil note : " I have seen another copy, but it was imperfect—G. N." On the title-page is written "William Shakespeare," apparently one of the Ireland forgeries.

The following entry occurs in Henslowe's Diary :—

" Received in earnest of Patient Grissell by us Tho. Dekker, Hen. Chettle and Willm. Hawton the sume of 3 li. of good and lawfull money by a note sent from Mr. Robt. Shaa's the 19th of December, 1599. By me,

Henry Chettle.

W. Haughton.

Thomas Dekker."

The Robert Shaa or Shaw here mentioned was, Mr. Collier tells us, one of the temporary managers of the company of the Earl of Nottingham's players. The comedy was entered at Stationers' Hall for publication on the 28th March, 1600, as " the Plaie of Patient Grissell," but it did not appear until three years afterwards.

The Pleasant Comodie of Patient Grissill. As it hath beene sundrie times lately plaid by the right honorable the Earle of Nottingham (Lord high Admirall) his servants. London. Imprinted for Henry Rocket, and are to be solde at the long shop under S. Mildred's Church in the Poultry, 1603. 4to. 42 leaves.

The play is anonymous, but the entry in Henslowe's Diary informs us who the authors were.

Patient Grissil: a Comedy by Thomas Dekker, Henry Chettle, and William Haughton. Reprinted from the Black-Letter edition of 1603, with an Introduction and Notes [by J. Payne Collier]. London. Printed for the Shakespeare Society. 1841. The introduction contains an interesting account of the history of Griselda.

On August 30th, 1667, Pepys saw at Bartholomew Fair the puppet play of "Patient Grizill," and Warton in a note to his *History of English Poetry* writes: "I need not mention that it is to this day represented in England on a stage of the lowest species and of the highest antiquity: I mean a puppet show."

"The Patient Countess," in Percy's *Reliques* from Warner's *Albions England*, is a totally different story from that of the patient wife of the Marquis Walter.

Warton mentions a MS. poem by William Forrest, and, as it has lately been printed, I give the title here, although it contains no notice of the original Grisild.

The History of Grisild the Second: a Narrative in Verse of the Divorce of Queen Katharine of Arragon. Written by William Forrest, sometime Chaplain to Queen Mary I., and now edited for the first time from the Author's MS. in the Bodleian Library by the Rev. W. D. Macray, M.A , F.S.A. London. Printed by Whittingham and Wilkins at the Chiswick Press, 1875. 4to. Roxburghe Club.

.The Griselda literature is a tolerably large one, and it is therefore scarcely necessary in this place to give more than the above general indication of an interesting subject. It may be noted that the titles of the works on the subject in the library of the British Museum occupy nine pages of the manuscript catalogue.

The patience of Griselda is almost as much a commonplace of literature as that of Job, and writers are full of references to her cruel fate. In a *Balade* translated by Lydgate from the Latin "Grisilde's humble patience" is recorded.

In Thomas Feylde's "Contraversye bytwene a Lover and a Jaye," printed without date by Wynkyn de Worde, we read :—

> " Ryght fewe of Grysyldes kynde
> Is now left on lyve."

We are told in *Harry White his Humour*, printed in 1660, that, "having lately read the rare history of Patient Grizell, out of it he hath drawne this phylosophicall position, that if all women were of that woman's condition we should have no imployment for cuckin-stooles."

The editor of the *Collection of Old Ballads*, 1723, slily remarks :—" It may naturally be supposed that he [the poet] had unfortunately married a shrew, and was willing to preach up the doctrine of patience to wives, by shewing them the blessings that attend this great uncommon virtue ; and I have inserted it, thinking that amongst my readers I might have some husbands who would be glad of carrying such an excellent song to their wives " (vol. i. p. 252).

Much of the popularity of the story must be due to Chaucer, who first introduced it to English readers and endued it with so much poetic beauty and grace.

THE

ANCIENT TRUE AND ADMIRABLE

HISTORY OF

PATIENT GRISEL,

A POORE MANS DAUGHTER IN FRANCE:

SHEWING

How Maides, By Her Example, In Their Good Behaviour
May Marrie Rich Husbands ;
And Likewise Wives By Their Patience And Obedience
May Gaine Much Glorie.

WRITTEN FIRST IN FRENCH, AND

Therefore to French I speake and give direction,
For English Dames will live in no subjection.

BUT NOW TRANSLATED INTO ENGLISH, AND

Therefore say not so, for English maids and wives
Surpass the French in goodnesse of their lives.

AT LONDON :

Printed by H. L. for William Lugger; and are to be sold at
his shop in Bedlem, neere Moore-Fields.

1619.

The Historie of Patient Grisel, made Marchionesse of Saluss, in which is Exemplified the true Obedience and Noble Behaviour of Vertuous Women towards their Husbands.

CHAP. I.

How the Marquesse of Saluss passed the time of his youth without any desire of mariage, till he was requested by the faire entreatie of a favorite, and other gentlemen, to affect a wife, both for the good of the country and the honour of himselfe; with his answer to the same.

Betweene the mountaines of Italy and France, towards the south, lyes the territory of Salus, a country flourishing with excellent townes and castles, and peopled with the best sort of gentles and peasants: amongst whom there lived not long since a nobleman of great hope and expectation, lord of the country, by name Gualter, Marquesse of Saluss; to whom, as the government appertained by right of inheritance, so their obedience attended by desert of his worthinesse.

He was young in yeeres, noble of lineage, and such attractive demeanour, that the best thought it a pleasure to bee commanded by him, and the worst grew more tractable by his good example : his delight was in hunting and hawking, and the pleasure of the time present extinguished the care of the time to come ; for he thought not of mariage, nor to entangle himselfe with the inconveniences of a wife ; till at last the people and noblemen of his country projected the contrary, as discontented to see him indisposed that way, and presaging a kind of prosperity to themselves, if by his mariage posteritie might arise to assure them the better how they might bestow their obedience hereafter. Whereupon they assembled together, and made one day amongst the rest a determiner of their resolutions, choosing out for their speaker a noble knight of great authority, faire demeanor, eloquent speech, and more inward with the Marquesse then any of the rest ; who, thus acquainted with all their mindes, and prepared to utter his owne minde, took an opportunity to acquaint the renowned Marquesse with the matter.

Most honourable Sir, the great humanity extended towards us, of which I most especially have participated, hath thus emboldened me above others, to make a further triall of your patience, and forbearing my rudeness : not that there is any sufficiency or singularity in me above others, but in that heretofore I have found you so generous toward all, I make no question to finde you as gratious toward my selfe ; and in that it hath pleased you to accept of our love, wee are proud againe to be under your obedience ; wherein we shall rejoice the more, if you now accord to our request the sooner, which is, to marry without delay. The time passeth, and will not be recalled, your youth intreats it, and must not be denied ; your country importunes it, and would not bee opposed ; your neighbours desire it, and hope to bee satisfied ; and all sorts request it, and wish it for your honour ; for when age approacheth, death attends it at the heeles, and no man can tell when, or how it will fall upon him. Therefore wee humbly request you to accept our supplications, and accord to this importunity, that we may provide by your appointment a lady worthy of your honour and our subjection. In this wee are the more suppliant, because it will rebound so much to the good of your countrey, and the enlarging your renowne ; for if it should so fall out (which God forbid) that you die without issue, we may lament the losse of our lord, but not redresse the complaints of the people : we shall want you that was al our comfort, but are sure of distresse to our everlasting trouble. If then you either love your selfe, or pity us, frame a heart to this impression, and leave not us to further feare and disquiet.

When the noble lord had thus apprehended the petition of his loving subjects, he resolved to answer them as gratiously as they had propounded the businesse with regard of duty, and so replied : My dearest friends, you have urged mee to a matter, in which as yet I have beene a mere stranger ; for by nature I delight in liberty, and by custome continued my pleasures, both which must needs bee curbed by mariage, and restrained by taking a wife : notwithstanding, I cast awaie all doubts to pleasure you, and will thinke of no incombrances so you be satisfied. For though mariage hath many difficulties attending ; especially, the feare of legitimation in our children, and suspicion of that honour which lies on our wives honesty, yet all shall be overcome with this resolution, that I shall please you in the same ; for I am resolved, if anie good come for man's contentment by mariage, it is from God, to whom I submit this cause, and pray for the goud successe of your wishes, that I may live to maintaine your peace, as well as my owne pleasure : and look, wherein my contentment shall enlarge mine honour, your welfare shall be respected above my life ; so that (beleeve it) I will satisfie your demands, and apply my selfe to the purpose. Only one thing I request at your hands ; to take in worth my choice, and neither insult if she be a princesse of greatnes, nor repine if she be of meane estate; but love her because I have loved you, and regard her howsoever in that she is my wife ; neither being curious nor inquisitive whom I will chuse, nor disaffected when it is past remedy.

When the company heard him out, and found him so willing to their satisfaction, they gave him thankes with one heart for his kinde admission, and answered with one tongue, he should not find them repugnant ; but they would honor his wife as the princesse of the world, and be morigerous to him as the commander of their soules. Thus did this new report (like a messenger of glad tidings) fill all the marquisate with joy, and the palace with delight, when they understood their lord would marry, and in a manner heard the time appointed ; for presently it was proclaimed through the countrey, and a day assigned for all commers to come to the court. The nobles prepared themselves in the best manner : the ladies spared no cost, either for ornaments of their bodies, or setting out their beauties ; the gentles flocked to please their lord, and were brave to set out their owne greatnes : the citisens were rich in their neatnes, and handsome in their attire : the officers were formall in their showes, and sumptuous in their attendants ; the countryman had his variety, and the verie peasant his bravery ; in a word, al sorts gloried in the hope of that festivall, and every man's expectation attended the day of triumph. For never was such a preparation in Saluss before, nor such a confluence of people seene in that countrey ; for besides the novelty, many forraine princes came to celebrate this mariage, and to shew their owne greatnes. Savoy was neare, and sent some from her snowie hills : France as neare, and sent others from her fruitful vines : Italy not far off, and sent many from her pleasant fields ; and the ilands round about kept none at home that would come. Thus were his kinred invited, strangers admitted, his owne people entertained, and all sorts welcommed ; but as yet no bride was seene, no woman named, no lady designed, no maid published, no wife knowne : onely the preparation was much, and the expectation greater.

All this while the Marquesse continued his hunting, and as he had accustomed, resorted much to a poore country village not farre from Salusse, where there dwelt as poore a countriman, named Janicole, overworne in yeares, and overcomne with distresse. But as it happens many times that inward graces doe moderate outward discommodities, and that God seasoneth poverty with contentment and their sufficient supportation, so had this poore man all his defects supplied in the admirable comfort of one onely daughter, so composed, as if nature determined a worke of ostentation. For such was her beauty in appearance, and vertue in operation, that it put judicious men to an extasie in the choice by comparison ; but both united did heere grace each other, and when they pretended an action, it was all to go forward to perfection. And whereas in others this temporary blessing gave wings to desire to bee seene and knowne abroad, in her those innated vertues allaied the heat of all manner of passion, and breakings out of frailty. The viands they had were but meane, and the diet they kept was to satisfie nature : the time was over-ruled by their stomachs, and the ceremonies they used were thanks to God, and moderation in their repasts. The utensiles of the house were homely, yet handsome in regard of their cleanlinesse : that bed which they had the ould man lay in, and the sweet daughter made shift with the ground. No day passed without prayers and praises to God (for was it not praiseworthy to have such grace in this disgrace), nor any night without taking account of the day passed.

Her exercise was to helpe her father in the morning, and drive forth her sheep in the day time: hee was at home making of nets, and shee abroad looking to her lambs : she was never heard to wish for any better, but to thank God it was no worse. No word of repining ever came from her mouth, or the least grudge from her heart : at night she folded her sheep and dressed her father's supper, then lay they downe to rest, and rested as' well as in a bed of downe indeed. This was the glory of their poverty, and memory of their contentment.

But as fire will not be hid where there is matter combustible, so vertue will not be obscured where there be tongues and eares : nor could the Marquesse so hallow after his hawks and hounds, but report hallowed in his eare as fast this wonderment ; insomuch that when it was confirmed by judicious relation he made it not dainty to be behoulding to his owne experience : which when he saw concurring with fame, the miracle brought a kinde of astonishment ; which continuing, the properties of such novelties, increased to meditation : and so comparing the rest with this rarity, he thought her a fit woman to make his wife, supposing that if she were vertuous by nature, she would not prove vicious by education ; but rather as a diamond is a stone of the same value whether set in lead or horne, it must needs be of more excellency embellished with gold and enamell. In which resolution hee prepared his heart, and went forward with his businesse.

In the meane time the Court was daintily furnished, the

plate prepared, the apparell magnificent, the coronet rich, the jewels precious, the ornaments exceeding, and all things befitting the magnificence of a prince and the dignities of a queen : only the nobles wondred, the ladies were amazed, the damsells marvelled, the gentles disputed, the people flocked, and all sorts attended to see who should possesse this wealth and bee adorned with these robes. Till at last the nuptial day came indeed : honour prepared the sumptuousness ; fame divulged the glory; hymen invited the guests ; magnificence adorned the roomes ; the officers marshald the state, and all looked for a bride ; but who she was the next chapter must discover.

CHAP. II.

How, after all this great preparation, the Marquesse of Saluss demanded Grisell of her poore father Janicola ; and, espousing her, made her Marchionesse of Saluss.

When all things were extended to this glorious shew, the Marquesse (as if he went to fetch his wife indeed) tooke with him a great company of earls, lords, knights, squires, and gentlemen, ladies, and attendants, and went from the palace into the countrey toward Janicolas house ; where the faire mayd Grisel, knowing nothing of that which hapned, nor once dreaming of that which was to come, had made her house and selfe somewhat handsome, determining (with the rest of her neighbour virgins) to see this solemnity : at which instant arrived the Marquesse with all his gracious company, meeting with Grisel as shee was carrying two pitchers of water to her poore fathers house. Of whom (calling her by her name) he asked where her father was ? She humbly answered, in the house. Goe then, said hee, and tell him I would speak with him. So the poore old man (made the poorer by this astonishment) came forth to the lord somewhat appauled, till the Marquesse, taking him by the hand, with an extraordinary chearefulnesse said, that he had a secret to impart unto him, and so, sequestering him from the company, spake these words :—Janicola, I know that you alwaies loved me, and am resolved that you doe not now hate me. You have been glad when I have been pleased, and will not now bee sorrowful if. I bee satisfied : nay, I am sure, if it lie in your power, you will further my delight, and not bee a contrary to my request. For I intend to begge your daughter for my wife, and bee your sonne in lawe for your advancement. What saiest thou, man ? wilt thou accept mee for a friend, as I have appointed thee for a father ?

The poore ould man was so astonished, that he could not looke up for teares, nor speak a word for joy ; but when the extasie had end, hee thus faintly replied :—My gracious soueraigne, you are my lord, and therefore I must accord to your will ; but you are generous, and therefore I presume on your vertue ; take her a Gods name, and make mee a glad father ; and let that God, which raiseth the humble and meek, make her a befitting wife, and fruitful mother. Why then, replied the Marquesse, let us enter your house, for I must ask her a question before you. So hee went in, the company tarrying without in great astonishment : the faire maid was busied to make it as handsome as she could, and proud againe to have such a guest under her roofe ; amazed at nothing but why hee should come so accompanied, and little conjecturing of so great a blessing approaching. But, at last, the Marquesse took her by the hand, and used these speeches :—To tell you this blush becomes you, it were but a folly ; and that your modesty hath graced your comlines, may prove the deceit of words, and unbefitting my greatnes ; but in a word, your father and I have agreed to make you my wife, and I hope you will not disagree to take me to your husband. For delay shall not intangle you with suspicion, nor two daies longer protract the kindnes ; onely I must be satisfied in this, if your heart afford a willing entertainement to the motion, and your vertue a constancy to this resolution, not to repine at my pleasure in any thing, nor presume on contradiction, when I determine to command. For as amongst good souldiers, they must simply obey without disputing the businesse : so must vertuous wives dutifully consent withoute reproofe, or the least contraction of a brow. Therefore be advised how you answer, and I charge you take heed, that the tongue utter no more then the heart conceits. All this while Grisel was wondring at the miracle, had not religion told her that nothing was impossible to the commander of all things ; which reduced her to a better consideration and thus brought forth an answere.

My gracious lord, I am not ignorant of your greatnesse, and know mine owne basenesse : there is no worth in me to be your servant, therefore there can be no desert to be your wife : notwithstanding, because God will be the author of miraculous accidents, I yeeld to your pleasure, and praise him for the fortune ; onely this I will be bold to say, that your will shall be my delight, and death shall be more welcome unto mee then a word of displeasure against you.

This is sufficient, answered the great lord, and so most lovingly he took her by the hand, and brought her to the company, even before all his peeres and great ladies, and told them she should bee his wife, so that wherein they extended their love, reverence, and obedience toward her, he could exemplifie his regard, care, and diligence toward them. And because outward shewes doe sometimes grace befitting actions (lest her poverty and basenes might too much daunt their expectation, and seeme disgratious to their noblenes), he commanded them with a morall livelinesse to adorne her with the richest robes they had; so that it was a pleasure to see how the ladies bestird themselves, a delight to behould the severall services performed, the many hands about her, the jewels and pendants, the robes and mantles, the ornaments and coronets, the collanaes and chaines, with all other particulars and accoustrements, but when she was apparelled indeed, it was a ravishment exceeding report, and they which stomached her preferment were now delighted with her glory. Such a benefit hath beauty by nature, and gratiousnesse by nurture.

Chap. III.

How the Marquesse and Grisel were married together.

After the ladies had thus adorned poore Grisel with robes befitting her estate, the Marquesse and all the noble company returned to Saluss, and in the Cathedrall Church, in sight of the people, according to the fulnesse of religious ceremonies, they were espoused together, and with great solemnitie returned to the palace. Herein yet consisted the admiration, that no word of reproach was murmured, nor eie looked unpleasantly upon her; for by her wonderfull demeanour shee had gained so much of opinion that the basenes of her birth was not thought upon, and all her graces concurring made them verely beleeve shee was extracted of princely lineage : no man once supposed that shee could be Grisel, daughter to poore Janicola, but rather some creature metamorphosed by the powers of heaven : for besides the outward statelinesse and majestical carriage of herselfe, the wonderfull modestie and exact symmetry of her countenance, the admirable beauty and extraordinary favor of her visage, her faire demeanour had a kinde of attraction, and her

gratious words a sweet delivery ; so that all that came to her
were glad of their accesse, and they which went from her
triumphed for their good speed : yea, report extended so far,
that she was not onely visited by her owne lords and ladies with
reverence, but attended on with strangers, who came from all
quarters to see her and to bee behoulding to their owne judgements ; so that if the Marquesse loved her before for her own
worth, he now reverenced her for others respect ; the rather,
because he found a blessing attending her presence, and all
people pleased in the contract ? For when any controversie
hapned betweene himselfe and his nobles, she was so nobly
minded, that what she could not obtaine by fair intreaty she
yet mitigated by sweet perswasion. When any unkindnes
hapned of forraine prince, shee urged those blessings of peace,
and reasoned the matter with delightsom enforcement ; and
when the people were either complained of, or against, he marvelled from whence she had those pretty reasons to asswage his
anger, and they verely beleeved shee was sent from heaven for
their releefe. Thus was shee amiable to her lord, acceptable to
her people, profitable to her country, a mirror of her sexe, a
person priviledged by nature, and a wonder of the time, in
which she did nothing out of time ; so that the Marquesse was
rather ravished than loving, and all his subjects resolved to
obedience from her good example.

Chap. IV.

How the lady Grisel was proved by her husband, who thus
made triall of her patience.

To other blessings, in processe of time, there was added the
birth of a sweet infant, a daughter, that rejoiced the mother,
and gladded the father : the country triumphed, and the people
clapped their hands for joy; for the Marquesse still loved her
more and more, and they thought their lives not deere for her,
if occasion served. Notwithstanding all this, Fortune hath still a
tricke to checke the pride of life, and prosperity must be sea-
soned with some crosses, or eke it would taint and corrupt us
too much : whereupon, the Marquesse determined now to
prove his wife, and make triall of her vertues indeed ; and so
taking a convenient season, after the childe was fully weaned,
he one day repaired secretly to her chamber, and (seeming halfe
angry) thus imparted his mind.

Although, Grisel, this your present fortune hath made you
forget your former estate, and that the jollity of your life over-
swayeth the remembrance of your birth, yet neither is it so

with me, nor my nobles; for I have some occasion of distasting, and they great cause of repining, in that they must be subject to one so base, and have still before their eyes our children of such low degree; so that though (for my sake) they make good semblance of the present, yet are they resolved never to suffer any of our posterity to rule over them; of which, as they have disputed with mee, I cannot chuse but forewarne you. Therefore, to prevent this discontentment betweene us, and to maintaine that peace which must corroborate my estate, I must needes yeelde to their judgements, and take away your daughter from you, to preserve their amity: the thing I know must be displeasing to nature, and a mother cannot well indure such a losse; but there is now no remedy: only make use of your first resolutions, and remember what you promised me at the beginning of our contract.

The lady, hearing this sorrowfull preamble, and apprehending the Marquesse resolution, to her griefe, (although every word might have beene as arrowes in her sides) yet admitting of the temptation, and disputing with herselfe to what end the vertues of patience, modesty, forbearance, fortitude, and magnanimity were ordained, if they had not subjects to worke upon, and objects to looke after, thus replyed.

My lord, you are my soveraigne, and all earthly pleasures and contentments of my life come from you, as the fountaine of my happinesse, and therefore please your selfe, and (beleeve it) it is my pleasure you are pleased; as for the child, it is the gift of God, and yours. Now he that gives may take away, and as wee receive blessings from heaven, so must we not dote on them on earth, lest by setting our minds too much upon them, wee cannot set off our hearts when they are taken from us; only one thing I desire, that you remember I am a mother; and if I burst not out into passion for her losse, it is for your sake I am no more perplexed, and so you shall ever find mee a wife befitting your desires.

When the Marquesse saw her constancy, and was in a manner pleased with her modest answere, hee replied not at all at that time; for his heart was full, and what betweene joy and feare he departed: joy that so great vertue had the increase of goodnesse, feare that he had presumed too farre on such a trial. But resolved in his businesse, hee went to put it to the adventure.

CHAP. V.

'The Marquesse sent a varlet for his daughter; but privately disposed of her with his sister, the Dutchesse of Bologna de Grace, who brought her up in all things befitting the childe of so great a person.

Not long after this sad conference between the Marquesse and his lady, hee called a faithfull servant unto him ; such a one as the poet talks of, *propter fidem et taciturnitatem dilectum*, to whom hee imparts this secrecy, and with severall instructions, what hee truly meant to do with the child, sent him to his wife with an unsavory message, which yet hee delivered in this manner.

I had not now come to you, most noble lady, though that power commanded me which hath my life in subjection, if I had not more relied upon your wisdome and vertue, than feared death it selfe. Therefore I crave pardon if I am displeasing in my message, and seeme cruell (as it were) in tearing your flesh from your sides, by bereaving you of this your daughter : for hee hath appointed it that must not bee gainsaid, and I am a messenger that cannot bee denied. But yet with what unwillingnes (God knowes my soule) in regard that you are so respected amongst us, that wee think of nothing but what may delight you, and talk not a word but of your merit and worthinesse.

When she had heard him out, remembring the conference the Marquesse had with her, and apprehending there was no disputing in a matter remedilesse, especially with a messenger, shee resolved it was ordained to dy; and although shee must now (as it were) commit it to a slaughter-house, whereby any woman in the world might with good becomming have burst out into some passion, and well enough shewed a distracted extasie, yet recollecting her spirits, and reclaiming those motives of nature already striving in her bowels, shee tooke the childe in her armes, and with a mothers blessing and sweetned kisses, the countenance somewhat sad, and the gesture without any violent excruciation, delivered it unto the fellow, not once amazed or distempred, because her lord would have it so, and shee knew not how to have it otherwise : only she said, I must, my friend, intreat one thing at your hands, that out of humanity and Christian observation, you leave not the body to bee devoured of beasts or birds, for it is worthy of a grave in her innocency, and Christian buriall, though shee were but my daughter alone.

The fellow having received the childe, durst not tarry for feare of discovery (such impression had her words made already), but returned with it to his maister, not leaving out the least circumstance of her answer, nor any thing that might enlarge her renown and constancy.

The Marquesse, considering the great vertue of his wife, and looking on the beauty of his daughter, began to enter into a kinde of compassion, and to retract his wilfulnesse; but at last resolution won the field of pity, and having (as he thought) so well begunne, would not so soone give over, but with the same secrecy hee had taken her from his wife, hee sent it away to his sister, the Dutchess of Bologna, with presents of worth, and letters of gratification, containing in them the nature of the businesse, and the manner of her bringing up, which she accordingly put in practice, receiving her neece with joy, and instructing her with diligence; so that it soone appeared under what a tutelage shee was, and whose daughter shee might be. For her pregnancy learned whatsoever they taught her, and the grace she added, quickly discovered that honour had confederated with nature to make her the offspring of such a mother.

Chap. VI.

'The Marquesse, not contented with this proofe, tooke away also her sonne, in which adversity (with other additions) she shewed an extraordinary patience.

After this tempest was overpast, the rage whereof might easily have broken the tender sides of poore Grisels barke (for shee verely beleeved that her daughter was slaine), the Marquesse still lay in waite for the trial of his wife, watching every opportunity which might acquaint him with her discontentments; especially if he might understand whether she complained of his rigorousnesse and unkindnesse, or no : but when he not only was advertised of her constancy and faire demeanour, but saw (by experience) that shee was neither elated in prosperity, nor dejected in adversity; when hee perceiued so great a temperature betweene the joy of her advancement and the sorrow for her trouble, he wondred at her constancy ; and the rather, because her love and observation toward him continued with that sweetnes, and had such delectable passages, that his heart was set on fire againe, and hee knew not how to allay the extreamities of his joy. In this manner passed foure yeeres, wherein she over-passed all of her kinde, and he thought it a donative from heaven to have such a wife. At last nature bestird herselfe againe, and made her a happy mother of a faire sonne; the joy whereof led the whole country into the house of praier and thanksgiving, and brought them home againe by cresset-light and bonfires, so that she well perceived how acceptable she was to her people and beloved of her husband. Notwithstanding, with the same water that drave the mill hee drowned it, and made her still beleeve the contrary; for after two yeeres, that the childe was past the danger of a cradle, and the trouble of infancy, he tooke occasion once againe to inflict upon the vertuous Grisel a new punishment, erecting his building upon the old foundation.

You knowe, saith hee, what former contentions I have had with my nobility about our marriage; not that they can lay any imputation on you or your worthy behavior, but on my fortune and disasterous affection to match myselfe so meanly: wherein yet their forward exprobation was rebated, all the while we either had no children, or that they supposed that which we had to be taken from us; all which ariseth out of the error of ambition (which in a manner is carelesse of vertue) respecting nothing but a high progeny. So that ever since this child was borne there hath passed many secret grudgings, and unkinde speeches against it, as if it were a disparagement to their great-nesse to have a lord of so meane parentage, and the country to be subject to the grand child of Janicola, whom you see never since our marriage they would admit to place of honor, or to overtop them by way of association, nor will suffer this my Gualter, though it carry the fathers name, to rule over them. Therefore, to allay the heat of these present fires, and to preserve the peace of my estate (by preventing the mischief of future troubles), I am resolved to settle my contentment, and to deale with your sonne as I have dealt with your daughter. And of this I thought it good to advertise you, as a preparative for patience, lest sorrow should distract you with oversuddennesse.

Now you ladies and dames of these times, that stand upon tearmes of spirit and greatnesse of heart (some will have it courage and magnanimity of minde), that are affrighted at the character of a foole, and silly poore soule; I speake not of strumpets, or of such as are willing to brand themselves with the impurity of uncleannesse, and dare out of impudency or cunning tell their husbands to their faces they will go where they list, and do what they please, but of such that under that impregnable target of honestie are yet so impatient at every distemperature, that they dare answer taunt for taunt: yea, like viragoes indeed, offer the first blow, though a horrible confusion follow, what would you have answered this lord? or with what fire-works would you have made your approches unto him? I will not tarry for your answere, lest I pull the old house in peeces, and so, though I scape the timber, I may be crushed with the rubbish; but I will now anticipate (or prevent) all

D

objections by telling you what faire Grisel said ; and if there bee hope of reformation, insert it as a caution to divert you from your naturall fiercenes.

When shee had heard him out, though to the griefe of her soule, she conceived the murther of her childe, and that the apprehension renewed the sorrow of her daughters losse ; yet would she give no way to such distemperature, that either hee should have cause to suspect her patience, or shee herselfe the temptation of disquiet, and therefore thus replied :—My lord, I have many times told you, that my soule rejoiceth in nothing but in your reposednes, for you are the lord of me and this infant ; and though I could bee contented to shew myselfe a mother in his education, and bring him now and then unto you as the pledge of our loves, yet are you the commander of my vowes, and I will rectifie all disordered appetites by the rule of your pleasure. Take him then, a Gods name, and if hee be marked for death, it is but the common brand of all creatures ; nay, if the mother may be a sacrifice of propitiation to appease your disquiet, never was lamb so meek, nor holocaust so willing to bee offred. For, what may bee comprehended under the titles of father, kinred, children, friends, life, pleasure, honours, and contentment, are all comprised under your love, and the society of a husband. Do with mee, then, what you please : the body shall serve your turne while it lives, and the soule attend you after death.

Here was an answer to pacifie the tyrants of Sicilie, and put a man quite out of his tract of proving such a wife! Yet the Marquesse onely made use of it to rejoice in the assurance of her goodness, and went the rather forward in his dangerous course of temptation.

CHAP. VII.

The Marquesse, resolute to prove his wife further, sendeth for his son, and disposeth of him as he had done of his daughter.

As this patient and wonderfull lady was one day sporting with her infant, like an untimely tempest (spoiling the beauty of some new rooted plants) did this messenger of death interpose himselfe betweene her recreation, making the hollow demand of her sonne worse than the noise of a schrich-owle over a sick mans bed : yet (as if there were a conscience in disquieting her greatnes, or if you will, her goodnes) he came forward with preambles and apologies, insinuating, with craving pardon, the authority of a lord, the duty of a servant, the terrour of death, the circumstance of obedience, and all other enforcements which might either excuse a messenger, or make the message of it selfe without blame.   What should I enlarge a discourse of terrour ? it is a curtesie to conclude a mischiefe with quicknes.   Hee was not so sudden in his demand, as shee was ready in her dispatch, for she presently blest the child,

kissed it, crossed it, adorned it, and delivered it to the execu-
tioner : onely with the same enforcement shee pleaded, as shee
had spoken of in the behalfe of her daughter, not to see it
perish for lack of a buriall, or devoured for want of a grave.

In this manner, and with this report, hee returned to his
lord, who had still more cause of amazement, and lesse reason
to trouble such a creature, had not his wilfulnes put him forward to make an end of his businesse, and taught him still
variety of trying this gold in the fire. But for the time hee
sent likewise this childe to his sister, the Duchesse of Bologna
(yet some will have her but Countesse of Paniche), who, understanding her brothers minde, brought up both these children in
such a fashion, that though no man knew whose children they
were, yet they imagined whose they might bee ; that is, the son
and daughter of some prince, or other potentate, willing to have
his children brought up to the best purpose, and befitting their
birth and honour.

The ordering of this businesse in this sort made the Marquesse once againe settle himselfe in Saluss, where he kept open
house to all comers, and was proud of nothing so much as the
honour of his wife, and the love of his people : for although he
had thus tried her patience and constancy, giving her more than
sufficient cause of anguish and perturbation, yet coulde he not
finde fault, or had the least demonstration of offence, but still
she loved him more and more, and was so observingly dutifull
and cautelous of displeasure, that many times he grew enamored

of that he might command, and seemed passionate in the dis-
tractions of over-joy. Nor could the length of time make this
love wearisome, for all they had lived thus a dozen years
together ; onely shee got the hand of him in the opinion of the
people, who by this beganne to whisper against his unkindnes,
that had married so vertuous a woman, and bereaved her of two
children ; so that if they were slaine, it was a murther, if
otherwise, it was unkindnesse. For though shee were poore
Janicolas daughter by birth, yet she might come from heaven
for her vertue, and was sure to go thither for her piety. Notwithstanding these breakings out, which came often to the eares
of his honour, such was her moderation and his government,
that they only whisperd the same on her behalfe, and contented
themselves with the expectation of future good, as they had the
fruition of present happinesse, not meddling with the same further,
than in the commiseration of her, and still acknowledging their
duty to him ; so that although hee knew shee might this way
understand his former reasons of taking away her children, that
it was but a devise, and that there were some other motives,
which procured this unkindnes, yet was he still obstinate to
exercise her patience, and conceit beat out another plot of
offence on the anvill of a loving, yet most hardned heart.

CHAP. IX.

The Marquesse, to try his lady further, made her beleeve hee
would marry another wife.

Some dozen years were passed since the Marquesse of Saluss
had sent his daughter to Bologna, to his sister (as you have
heard), who was by this time growne to that beautie, comelinesse,
and perfection, that her fame busied all Europe; and the lady
Grisel, her mother, was made acquainted with her excellency,
whereupon, he very strangely sent to Rome, by a messenger of
trust, for counterfeit letters to marrie [t]his paragon, and to bee
dispensed from his first wife. Which was so effectually dispatched,
that the messenger soone returned with the approbation of his
request, and hee himselfe had many allegations in readinesse to
excuse the matter, intimating the good of the countrie, and the
continual desire of his people for the alteration; which, although
it was far from probability, because they pitied their ladies distresse, and rather repined against their lords inconstancy, yet it
served his turne for the time, and he thereupon erected the
frame of this second marriage. By this time is the faire Grisel

acquainted with the businesse, and troubled at the misfortune; but having many times plaied the wanton with affliction, she resettled herself to endure whatsoever should be imposed; so that when she came to the proofe, indeed, nothing affronted her constancy nor humbled her lower then her own vertue had taught her the way.

In the mean while, the Marquesse had under hand sent to the Count of Paniche and his sister, to bring him his children with all the pompe and glory they could prepare, with caution not to discover their names, and to be at a day appointed at Saluss : so that it passed for current all over the country that a lady, a yong, brave, and gallant lady, of great lineage, and greater worth, of high renown and mighty affinity, was comming into Saluss to be espoused to the Marquesse, and that they were already come out of Bologna de Grace, a whole dayes journey forward, with such a troope and company that it was a shew of magnificence, and a spectacle of delight. For amongst the rest there was a young lord, not fully eight yeere old, whose bravery and gallantnesse drewe all mens eyes with admiration toward him, had not the lady divided the gazing, and shared with their opinion. For, besides her riches and outward ornaments, her youth (as not fully thirteene) and upright comelinesse, her bewty and gracious behauiour, she was of extraordinary stature, and majestike presence.

These things thus disposed and handsomely carried, the Marquesse tooke an opportunity thus to speak to the disconsolate

Grisel before all his people. In times past, I confesse, you deserved my love, and notwithstanding the disparity betweene us, I thought it well bestowed upon you; nay, I cannot now impute any ill desert unto you: notwithstanding, for some reasons to myselfe best knowne, of which I have made the holy father acquainted, I am resolved to take another wife; who, as you heare, is on the way hitherward already: wherefore I would advise you to retire to your fathers cotage, till you heare further from me.

Alas! my lord, replied the sweet soule, I ever disputed the matter with reason, that there was no equality betweene so great magnificence and my humiliation, and in the greatest assurance of my prosperity, reputed my selfe a vassaile and handmaid, proud of nothing but my owne readinesse to be at your command, and your willingnes to employ mee in your affaires; so that, I take God to my witnes, I scarce trusted my selfe with the name of a wife, when I was in the best assurance. Therefore, I must acknowledge what you have heretofore vouchsafed as a part of great bounty, and the very fruits of your generousnes. As for returning to my poore fathers house, I am most willing; and there, as you please, like a forlorne widow will spend the rest of my dayes; yet remember I was your wife, espoused orderly, and you have had children by mee, so that if I there dye, I must yet dye the widow of such a lord, and for honors sake be so reputed. As for your new spouse, God grant her many daies of comfort, and you

E

many yeeres of joy, that you may live in reciprocall delight one with another, and intertaine no worse contentment than poore Grisel accustomed. As for my dowry I brought, I brought only my selfe, and will have no more back againe, which was faith, love, reverence, poverty and virginity; for, as I came naked from my fathers house, I am contented to return so againe. Your jewels are in the wardrobe, and even the ring you married me withal, in the chamber: of this I weare, I shall quickly be disrobed, and if there be any further misery appointed, my patience can endure it, if your pleasure impose it; onely in recompence of my virginitie, I request a poore smocke to hide that wombe from public overlooking that was once so private to so great a prince; and because it was the bed of your infants, let it not bee the scorne of your people, but give mee leave thus to goe out of the palace, that hereafter times may wonder how quietly a woman yeelded to so great a change. Nay, let no man shed a teare, I must bee more naked than so; for though the wife of a Marquesse while I lived, and the widow when I died, yet am I not too good for a grave, but in despight of pride must return to dust and ashes.

Did I say before, they began to weep? I can assure you, when she had done, they roared out-right; yea, the Marquesse himselfe shed so many teares that he was faine to retire, and commanded the smock she had begged to be sent unto her, that shee might prosecute the enterprise, and he determine his businesse, as he had constantly projected.

Chap. VIII.

How the patient Grisel was disrobed of her apparell, and restored all she had (except one poore smocke) to the Marquesse.

Before I proceed any further in this wonderfull discovery, I am sure two things will bee objected against mee: first, the impossibility of the story ; secondly, the absurdity of the example. For the story I answer, that therefore it was thus published and connected together, for the rarity of the businesse, and the sweetnes of the successe, nor is it any way stranger than many Roman passages, and Grecian discourses. For the application, it is both necessary and befitting ; for whereas in the condition of women, amongst many other, there bee two especiall errours against the modesty of their sex, and quietnes of their husbands, videlicet, superiority and desire of liberty (I name not irregular behaviour, household inconveniences, and domesticks strife), this one example (as Hercules did the serpents) strangles them both in the cradle, and though it cannot prevent, yet will it exprobrate the fault.   First concerning superiority. I hope the instances of scripture are not made canonicall to no purpose, and out of reason and naturall inforcement : what a filthinesse is it to a generous spirit, to have a woman so presumptuous as to take an account of her husband's actions and businesse ? Wherein many times they are so peremptory, that I have seene them enter the rooms of privacy, where secret businesses of strangers have been imparted, and were to be discussed, nor hath this been done with a lovely insinuation, or cunning excuse of longing, or willingness to be instructed, or other pretty inducements to permission, but with a high commanding voice, and impudent assurances of their owne worth : yea, I have knowne them breake open letters before they came to their husbands' overlooking, and have wondred even at souldiers themselves, that would give way to such indecency. Againe, to be counter-checked in this wilfulnes, what clamours have beene raised ! what tumults and discomforts occasioned ! that instead of awful obedience and delightsome affability, they have burst out into outragiousnes, commanded teares of mischeife, and threatned suspicious revenges. But let them soile themselves in the filthinesse of this humour never so much. I say plainely, that though their husbands were fooles by nature, yet is it not befitting for a wife to discover the same, or over-rule in forren affaires, I meane matters which concerne them not : for there is no great man so weake but hath councell and supportation of inferior officers, nor mean man so sottish but hath friends or servants in the dispatch of his businesse. Secondly, concerning the desire of liberty : oh, hellish device of the divell, and fearefull custome both of France and England! I hope he that knowes the fashions of the East, of Muscovy, Spain, Italy, and the Mores, understands that no married wife goes abroad but to honorable purposes; and it is an introduction to death to salute any stranger, or be seene in private conference. For, in true understanding, what businesse should any man have with my wife three houres together in private? or why, without my leave, and that upon good grounds, should shee wander in publike? I speake not to overthrow noble societies, generous entertainment, familiar invitations, curteous behaviour, charitable welcomes, honest recreations, or peradventure, the imparting of private businesse; but meerly against foppish wantonesse, idle talke, suspicious meetings, damnable play-hunting, disorderly gaming, unbefitting exercises, and in a word, all such things as tend to obscenity and wickednes; in which (say what women can), if there be not a moderation by nature, there must be an inforcement by judgement; and that woman that will not be ruled by good councell must be over-ruled by better example,—of which, this now in hand (of Lady Grisel) is a mirror, and transparent chrystall to manifest true vertue, and wifely duty indeed; and so I come to the wonder of her obedience.

After the Marquesse was resolved to the last act of her tryall, and had sent her the smocke shee demanded, amongst all the lords, knights, ladies, and other company, she presently disrobed

her selfe, and went, so accompanied, from the palace to her
father's cottage, who, as you have heard (for divers reasons),
was only kept from want, but never advanced out of the same.

The company could not choose but weepe and deplore the
alteration of fortune ; she could not choose but smile, that her
vertue was predominant over passion : they exclaimed against
the cruelty of her lord, she disclaimed the least invective against
him : they wondred at so great vertue and patience, she resolved them they were exercises befitting a modest woman :
they followed her with true love and desire to doe her good,
she thanked them with a true heart, and request to desist from
any further deploring of her estate.

By this time they approached the house, and the poore old
man, Janicola, acquainted with the hurli-burly, came out to see
what the matter was. And finding it was his daughter in her
smocke, and in so honourable a company, bemoaning her distresse, he quickly left them all unspoke unto, and ran in for
those poore robes, which were formerly left in the house ; with
which hee quickly arayed her, and told her before them all,
that now shee was in her right element, and, kissing her, bad
her welcom. The company was as much astonished at his
moderation as at her constancie, wondring how nature could
bee so restrained from passion, and that any woman had such
grace to be so gracious; in which amaze, not without some
reprehension of fortune, and their lord's cruelty, they left her
to the poverty of the cell, and returned themselves to the glory

of the palace, where they recounted to the Marquesse the strangenesse of the businesse, and the manner of the accidents, and shee continued in her first moderation and indefatigable patience, the poore father onely laughing to scorne the miseries and sodaine mutabilitie of humane condition, and comforting his daughter in her well-begun courses of modesty and reposed-nesse.

Not long after approched the Countesse of Paniche, or, if you will, Duchesse of Bologna, with her glorious company and beautifull lady, sending word before hand that she would be at Saluss such a day : whereupon the Marquesse sent a troope to welcome her, and prepared the court for her intertainment ; the bruit of which yet had not so equall a passage, but divers contrarious opinions thus bandied themselves ; some absolutely condemnied the inconstancie of the lord, others deplored the misfortune of the lady, some repined to see a man so cruell against so great worthinesse, others exemplified her praises to all eternitie ; some were transported with the gallant youth and comelinesse of this new bewtifull virgine, others presumed to parallell the faire Grisel, but that shee had stepped a little before her in yeeres ; some harped upon her great nobilitie and high lineage, others compared the former wife's vertue and true wisdome ; some excused their lord, by the love to his countrey, others excused the lady by the nature of the adversitie, untill the approach of the faire virgine and the young noble man in her company extinguished all former conceits, and set them to a new worke, concerning this spectacle, wherein the young lady and her brave brother had such pre-eminence. Nor knewe the Earle of Paniche himselfe, or any of the company on either side, that they were his owne children by Grisel, but meerly strangers, and designed for this new mariage. So the great Marquesse made good semblance, and with his accustomed courtlinesse welcomed them all to the palace.

The very next morning (or, if you will, the day before), he sent a messenger for Grisel to come unto him in the very same manner as shee was ; who protracted no time, but presently attended her lord : at her approach he was somewhat appalled, but yet setting (as wee say) the best foot forward, hee thus proceeded:

The lady, Grisel, with whom I must marrie, will bee here to-morrow by this time, and the feast is prepared accordingly: now, because there is none so well acquainted with the secrets of my palace, and disposition of my selfe as you, I would have you, for all this base attire, address your wisdome to the ordering of the businesse, appointing such officers as is befitting, and disposing the roomes according to the degrees and estate of the persons. Let the lady have the priviledge of the mariage chamber, and the young lord the pleasure of the gallery: let the rest be lodged in the courts, and the better sort upon the sides of the garden : let the viands be plentifull, and the ceremonies maintained : let the showes bee sumptuous, and the pastimes as it becommeth ; in a word, let nothing be wanting, which may set forth my honour, and delight the people.

My lord, saith shee, I ever told you I took pleasure in nothing but your contentment, and whatsoever might consort to your delight, therein consisted my joy and happinesse : therefore, make no question of my diligence and duty in this, or any other thing which it shal please you to impose upon me. And so like a poore servant shee presently addressed herselfe to the businesse of the house, performing all things with such a quicknes and grace that each one wondred at her goodnesse and faire demeanour, and many murmured to see her put to such a triall. But the day of entertainement is now comme, and when the faire lady approached, her very presence had almost extinguished the impression of Grisels worthinesse ; for some inconstant humourists gave way to the alteration, not blaming the Marquesse for such a change. But when the strangers were made acquainted with the fortune of Grisel, and saw her faire demeanour, they could not but esteeme her a woman of great vertue and honour, being more amased at her patience then at the mutability of mans conditions ; till at last shee approached the lady, and taking her by the hand, used this speech.

Lady, if it were not his pleasure, that may command to bid you welcome, yet me thinks there is a kinde of over-ruling grace from nature in you, that must exact a respect unto you.

F

And as for you, yong lord, I can say no more, but if I might
have my desires satisfied in this world, they should be imploied
to wish you well, and to endeavour all things for your entertainement indeed.   To the rest I afford what is befitting,
desiring them, that if any deficiency abate their expectation,
they would impute it either to my ignorance, or negligence;
for it is the pleasure of him, in whose will is all my pleasure,
that in all sufficiency you should have regard and suppliment.
And so shee conducted them to their severall chambers, where
they reposed themselves awhile, till the time of dinner invited
them to repast.   When all things were prepared, and the
solemnity of placing the guests finished, the Marquesse sent
for Grisel, and rising on his feet, took her by the hand before
them all, erecting his body, and elating his voice in this manner:
You see the lady is heere I meane to marry, and the company
gloriously prepared to witnes the same ; are you therefore contented that I shall thus dispose of my selfe, and do quietly
yeeld to the alteration ?

My lord, replied she before them all, wherein as a woman I
might be faulty, I will not now dispute; but because I am your
wife, and have devoted my selfe to obedience, I am resolved to
delight in nothing but your pleasure; so that if this match be
designed for your good, and determined by your appointment, I
am much satisfied, and more then much contented.   And for
you, lady, I wish you the delights of your marriage and the
honour of your husband, many yeares of happinesse, and the

fruits of a chaste wedlock: only, gracious lord, take heed of one thing; that you trie not this new bride as you have done your ould wife; for she is yong, and peradventure of another straine, and so may want of that patience and government which I, poore I, have endured.

'Till this he held out bravely; but nature overcomming resolution, and considering with what strange variety his unkindnesse had passed, hee could not answere a word for teares, and all the company stood confounded at the matter, wondring what would be the end of the businesse, and the successe of the extasie. But to draw them out of their doubts, the next chapter shall determine the controversie.

CHAP. X.

The oration of the Marquesse to his wife, and the discovery of her children, to her great joy, and the contentment of all the company.

After a little reducement of his passion, and that time and further meditation had disposed his senses to their perfect estate, the Marquesse graciously answered:—

Thou wonder of women, and champion of true vertue! I am ashamed of my imperfections, and tyred with abusing thee. I have tryed thee beyond reason, and thou hast forborne mee beyond modestie : beleeve it, therefore, I will have no wife but thy selfe, and when God hath thought thee too good for the earth, I will (if it bee not too much superstition) pray to thee in heaven. Oh ! 'tis a pleasure to be acquainted with thy worth, and to come neere thy goodnes maketh a man better than himselfe. For without controversie, except thou hadst beene sent from above, thou couldst never have acted a god-desses part belowe: and therefore, seeing I have used thee so

unkindly heeretofore, I protest never to disquiet thee heereafter:
and wherein my cruelty extended against thee in bereaving thee
of thy children, my love shall now make amends in restoring
thy daughter. For this new bride is shee; and this wanton her
brother. Thank this great lady (my sister) for their bringing
up, and this man (you knowe him well enough) for his secrecy.
Bee not amased at the matter: I have related a truth, and will
confirme it on my honour; only sit downe till the dinner is
done, and bid the company welcome in this poore attire; for
the sun will break through slender clouds, and vertue shine in
base array. I could much dilate the matter, but it is time to
end, lest the circumstances will never end.

This device of the Marquesses, of kissing her so lovingly,
and setting her downe by him so discreetly, did much good; for
the company had time to dispute of the miracle, and the yong
lady reason to prepare her obedience; which, no sooner was the
dinner finished, but shee as soone performed, nothing thought
upon but joy at the matter, and wonder at the accident; every
one pleased to see such a unity of goodnes, and all delighted to
have a businesse so well concluded. But seeing time had un-
clasped a booke of such jollity, there was now no further disputing, for the ladies flocked about her to attend her into the
chamber, where the yong princesse her daughter was as ready
as the best to apparell her, so that when shee came amongst
them againe she shined like the sun after a tempest, and seemed

more glorious, because her continued modesty kept her from all insulting and vaine-glorious bravery.

Thus was the Marquesse invested, as it were, with a new blessednes, and she continued in her ould constancy; onely admired by every one for her patience and sufferings, and all aplauding their reconcilement, blessing her, and the people proud they had such a lord to obey : especially satisfied when the poore Janicola was advanced to the councell, and made governor of his palace ; wherein hee behaved himselfe so well that for ten yeares hee still lived as he had beene bred, a courtier, and died with the memory of a good report. Grisel lasted thirty yeares after him, and all went to their graves in good time, the country renowned over the world for their admirable government, and famosed for their extraordinary wonder.

Non est ulla difficultas (ut ita dicam) neque passio, neque cala-mitas dira, cujus non sufferre queat pondus hominis natura. —
Euripides Orestei.

FINIS.

www.ingramcontent.com/pod-product-compliance
Lightning Source LLC
Chambersburg PA
CBHW021536270326
41930CB00008B/1275